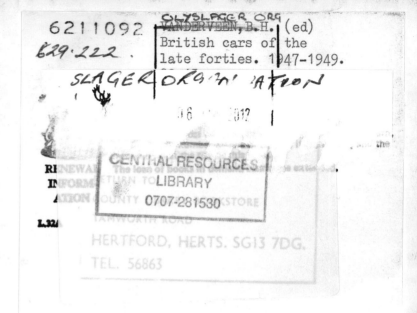

OLYSLAGER AUTO LIBRARY

British Cars of the Late Forties 1947-1949

compiled by the OLYSLAGER ORGANISATION
edited by Bart H. Vanderveen

FREDERICK WARNE & Co Ltd
London and New York

THE OLYSLAGER AUTO LIBRARY

This book is one of a growing range of titles on major transport subjects.
Titles published so far include:

The Jeep
Half-Tracks
Scammell Vehicles
Fire-Fighting Vehicles
Earth-Moving Vehicles
Wreckers and Recovery Vehicles
Passenger Vehicles 1893–1940
Buses and Coaches from 1940
Fairground and Circus Transport

American Cars of the 1930s
American Cars of the 1940s
American Cars of the 1950s

British Cars of the Early Thirties
British Cars of the Late Thirties
British Cars of the Early Forties
British Cars of the Late Forties

Library of Congress Catalog Card No. 73-89828

ISBN 0 7232 1756 4

Filmset and printed in Great Britain
by BAS Printers Limited, Wallop, Hampshire

636.973

INTRODUCTION

The late 1940s was a period of immense effort by the British car industry. Firstly the manufacturers had to get their car production back into top gear—an activity which was hampered by an acute steel shortage. Secondly they had to spend much time and capital on introducing new, modernized models.

Most of the 1945/46 cars, which are covered in the companion volume, *British Cars of the Early Forties (1940–46)*, were carry overs from 1940 and before; these remained in production, with relatively minor changes, until well into 1948. During this time the real post-war models were designed and developed, but when these eventually emerged the majority were sold abroad, earning badly-needed foreign currency. Some of the new cars which were released for sale at home found their way to a flourishing black market—'slightly used' cars being resold as second-hand for considerable profits. A Covenant scheme was then devised whereby a new car had to remain in the first owner's hands for at least one year (later two).

An important factor in post-war British car design was the abolition of the crippling RAC-rating horsepower tax. From January 1947, cars registered for the first time were taxed on the basis of cylinder cubic capacity, and in 1948 came a new flat-rate road tax system: £10 annually for any type of four-wheeled car. This had an almost immediate effect on engine design, encouraging larger piston area and shorter stroke, replacing the slow-revving long-stroke units of the thirties. By the end of the forties production of the typical Eights, Tens, Twelves, etc. had ceased, and British cars got a totally new image, especially overseas, where they could now be sold really competitively. Some of the cars which appeared in 1948/49 were extremely successful, particularly the Morris Minor (designed during the war and produced until the early 1970s) and, at the other end of the scale, the Jaguar XK120 which needs no further comment.

Another very successful vehicle introduced during this period was the Land-Rover which now—25 years and 850,000 units later—is still in production in fundamentally the same form. A noteworthy point here is that its current military version, evolved in the late 1960s, looks much like the war-time 'Jeep', from which the original Land-Rover was a direct development, the wheel having turned full circle in about two decades!

Piet Olyslager MSIA, MSAE, KIVI

1947

Most British 1947 models were carryovers from 1946, and 1946 models, in turn, were in most cases similar, if not identical, to those of 1939/40. Notable exceptions were the AC, Allard, Armstrong Siddeley, Austin Sheerline and Princess, Bristol, Healey, Jowett Javelin, Lagonda, MG 1¼-Litre, Riley 1½- and 2½-Litre and Triumph 1800, but most of these were limited-production models. Total car production was 287,000, the majority coming from the plants of Austin, Ford, Nuffield (MG, Morris, Riley, Wolseley), Rootes (Hillman, Humber, Sunbeam-Talbot), Standard (Standard, Triumph) and Vauxhall.

There were 147,767 new car registrations in the UK, as well as 7,847 new 'hackneys'. 140,691 cars were exported and 222 imported. Not until 1954 would the number of exports surpass the home sales number again and imports remained low until the late 1950s.

Prices quoted in this section are those valid in August 1947, and inclusive of purchase tax, unless stated otherwise. Certain makers offered 'bare' chassis, listed at basic price, the purchase tax amount being calculated on the completed car.

A typical English home, but a distinctive English car

4A AC 2-Litre

4A: **AC** Cars Ltd of Thames Ditton in Surrey, launched their new post-war model in March 1947. Apart from the pre-war 15·7 HP 1991-cc (65 × 100 mm) OHC engine it was entirely new and the Saloon as shown remained in production, with periodical detail improvements, until 1956. The brakes were Girling hydro-mechanical, i.e. hydraulic front and mechanical rear with 12-in drums and the suspension was conventional (non-independent) with leaf springs front and rear. Wheelbase was 9 ft 9 in and the engine, which had three SU carburettors and an output of 74 bhp, drove through a four-speed gearbox. Price £1277.

4B Allard J1

4B: **Allard** Motor Company Ltd of Clapham High Street, London SW4, offered three models, namely the Model L four-seater Tourer, the Model K1 two-seater Roadster and the Model J1 two-seater Sports (shown). The standard engine was the 3·6-litre Ford V8 of 85 or 95 bhp, but for the J1 a larger-bore (81- v. 77·8-mm) 3·9-litre variant with overhead valves, two Solex carburettors and a power output of 140 bhp was available. In July the Model M Drop-Head Coupé appeared. The K1, L and M models remained in production until 1949.

5A Alvis Fourteen

5B Armstrong Siddeley Lancaster

5C Austin Ten

5A: **Alvis** Fourteen, Model TA14, was available in chassis and
complete four-door Saloon form, the latter at £1276. Introduced in
1946, the Saloon was continued until 1950. Powered by a four-
cylinder 1·9-litre (1892-cc, 74 × 110 mm) 65-bhp engine with one
SU carburettor, the car was of conventional but sturdy and elegant
design. It had a four-speed gearbox and rigid axles with semi-elliptic
leaf springs. An unusual feature was the possibility of adjusting the
tubular-type bumper mounting brackets, maximum gap between bumper
and body providing increased protection.

5B: **Armstrong Siddeley** Lancaster 16 HP four-door six-light Saloon
was in production from late 1945. Other body styles on the same
9 ft 7 in wheelbase chassis were the Hurricane Drophead Coupé
(also from November 1945) and the Typhoon two-door Saloon
(from August 1946). All three were produced until September 1949
when several modifications were introduced including a larger-bore
engine (2309-cc v. 1991-cc). Both engines were OHV sixes. The
model names were those of famous aircraft produced during the war
by the Hawker Siddeley combine. Prices ranged from £1247 to £1272.
5C: **Austin** Ten Saloon, Model GS1, was the same as in 1946 and
discontinued in October 1947. A sliding roof was optional. This
specimen was photographed at Bombay Airport, India, alongside a
1947 Chevrolet Fleetmaster. In the background is a Commer Commando
air passenger coach of the BOAC.

1947

6A Austin Twelve

6A : **Austin** Twelve Saloon, Model HS1, was similar to the Sixteen (*q.v.*) with the main exception of the engine which was a 1535-cc 40-bhp side-valve Four. Both cars had 8 ft 8½ in wheelbase. This well-kept LHD model was seen in Spain in 1966.

6B : **Austin** Sixteen Countryman, Model BW1, was introduced in late 1947 and offered until 1949, but relatively few were made. Apart from the bodywork it was similar to the 16 HP Saloon (Model BS1) with the 2·2-litre OHV Four engine. Other four-cylinder Austin cars in 1947 were the Eight (AS1), Ten (GS1) and Twelve (HS1); all three were superseded in October by the new A40 Devon and Dorset models (*see* 1948).

6B Austin Sixteen

Current Austins comprise 8, 10, 12 and 16 h.p. de-luxe, 4-door, 4-cylinder sliding head saloons, priced from £280 to £525. Also the '110' Sheerline and '120' Princess 6-cylinder saloons, priced at £1,000 and £1,350 respectively. All the above prices are subject to Purchase Tax.

more and more people are saying...

AUSTIN - you can depend on it!

6C Austin A110 Sheerline

6C : **Austin** announced two entirely new six-cylinder models in March 1947, viz. the 3½-litre A110 Sheerline (110 bhp, single Stromberg carb.) and A120 Princess (120 bhp, triple SU carbs). Soon afterwards the engine size was increased from 3460 to 3993 cc and these 4-litre models were designated A125 Sheerline and A135 Princess. The few 3½-litre cars which by this time had been produced were retrofitted with the new engine. The A110 Sheerline with its large Lucas P100 headlamps is shown here. The Princess had coachwork by Vanden Plas with built-in headlamps and more flowing lines (*see* 1948).

7A Bentley 4¼-litre Mark VI

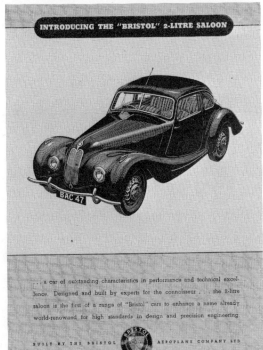

INTRODUCING THE "BRISTOL" 2-LITRE SALOON

BAC 47

. . . a car of outstanding characteristics in performance and technical excellence. Designed and built by experts for the connoisseur . . . the 2-litre saloon is the first of a range of "Bristol" cars to enhance a name already world-renowned for high standards in design and precision engineering.

BUILT BY THE BRISTOL AEROPLANE COMPANY LTD

7B Bristol 400

7A: **Bentley** 4¼-Litre Mark VI, 'the Silent Sports Car', was available in chassis form (at £1985 basic) and as Saloon (shown, £4038 incl. PT). In addition there were a Drophead Coupé by Park Ward and Saloons by Mulliner and Young, priced at up to £5456. They were powered by an F-head (inlet-over-exhaust) 4275-cc (89 × 114 mm) Six engine, the power output of which was not disclosed. Wheelbase was 10 ft.

7B: **Bristol** 400 was built by the Bristol Aeroplane Company and had been developed in conjunction with AFN Ltd of Frazer-Nash-BMW fame. The Bristol's radiator grille was similar to that of the German BMW and the engine was developed from the pre-war BMW 328. The 400 was offered until the early 1950s by which time it had already been joined by two restyled models, the 401 and 402.

7C: **Daimler** Straight-Eight DE36 chassis with eight-passenger Landaulette coachwork by Hooper. Daimler supplied the DE36, as well as the DE27 six-cylinder shorter-wheelbase variant, only in chassis form, at basic prices of £2025 and £1700 respectively; the bodywork was produced and fitted by specialist coachbuilders such as Freestone & Webb, Hooper and Windover. The 4·1- and 5½-litre engines had identical bore and stroke, namely 85·09 × 120·015 mm. Daimler also offered a complete 2½-Litre Saloon, Model DB18, as well as a Barker-bodied Drophead Coupé, both on a 9 ft 6 in wheelbase chassis.

7C Daimler Straight-Eight

1947

8A: Ford continued production of their successful 8 HP Anglia (EO4A) and 10 HP Prefect (E93A) models which had first been introduced shortly before the war. In 1948 they sold at £293 and £352 respectively. The Prefect (shown) had basically the same 92·5-mm stroke four-cylinder SV engine as the Anglia, but the bore was 63·5 instead of 56·6 mm. Both had a three-speed gearbox, torque-tube transmission and transversal leaf springing front and rear. Commercial van derivatives of these two cars were the 5-cwt E04C and 10-cwt E83W respectively. Later in the year the V8 Pilot Saloon was introduced (*see* 1948).

8B: Healey offered two models on a common 8 ft 6 in wheelbase chassis with trailing arm IFS and coil springs front and rear. Shown is the H2·4 two-door Elliott Saloon, the other body style being a two-door four-seater Roadster. The engine was a 2443-cc (80·5 × 120 mm) OHV Four with twin SU carburettors, 6·97:1 CR and a maximum power output of 104 bhp.

9: Hillman Minx Saloon was a carryover from 1946 and sold at £474 (DeLuxe). The car had an integral welded body-cum-chassis structure and conventional suspension with semi-elliptic leaf springs front and rear. The Minx as shown, later known as Mk I, was in production from August 1945, until December 1947.

8A Ford Prefect

8B Healey 2·4-Litre

9 Hillman Minx

1947

10A Hillman Minx

10B HRG

11 : **Humber** Pullman Mk I was produced from August 1945, until May 1948, with virtually unchanged specification. Illustrated is a Landaulette modification of the Limousine. This modification entailed complete conversion of the rear end and was one of two ordered from Rootes by the Government of Southern Rhodesia for the forthcoming Royal Tour.

10C Humber Super Snipe

10A: **Hillman** Minx Drophead Coupé, an attractive variant selling at £557. An Estate car was also offered, based on the Commer light van (itself a derivative from the Minx).

10B: **HRG** Sports two-seaters were available with either 1074-cc or 1496-cc OHC four-cylinder engine, the cars being designated 1100 and 1500 respectively. The two models were almost identical in appearance. The basic engines were made by Singer but modified in many respects, especially in the case of the 1500. Wheelbase was 8 ft 4½ in

for the 1100, 3 in more for the 1500. Prices were £812 and £968, and an Aerodynamic coupé variant was offered at £1247.

10C: **Humber** continued their three 1946 Saloons, the Hawk at £799, the Snipe at £991 and the Super Snipe at £1017. The Hawk had a four- the other a six-cylinder engine. They all had the same bodyshell and general appearance. The Hawk had steering-column gear change from September 1947 (Mk II). Illustrated is a Super Snipe at the Swan Barracks in Perth, Australia.

11 Humber Pullman

12A Jaguar

12A: **Jaguar** offered two basic Saloon models, viz. the 9 ft 4½ in wheelbase four-cylinder 1½-Litre (1776 cc, 73 × 106 mm) with single SU carburettor and the 10 ft wheelbase six-cylinder with 2664-cc (2½-Litre) or 3485-cc (3½-Litre) twin-carb. engine. The 2½-Litre had the same bore and stroke as the 1½-Litre, and those of the 3½-Litre were 82 and 110 mm. All models had overhead valves, four-speed gearboxes and 18-in wire wheels. They were produced from late 1945 until 1949. 1947 prices ranged from £865 to £1199.

12B: **Jowett** Cars Ltd of Bradford had introduced their attractive and rather unconventional Javelin Saloon in 1946 and commenced quantity production in mid-1947. The fast-back six-light body offered accommodation for up to six people and was mounted on a relatively long wheelbase, making it possible to have square-bottom rear doors. The gearshift lever was mounted on the steering column and the engine was a 1486-cc 50-bhp flat-four with overhead valves and two Zenith carburettors. The radiator was behind the engine. Note the optional 'transparent plastic half-roof' featured in this September 1947 advertisement.

12C: **Lagonda** 2½-Litre Mk 1 cars were made from September 1946, until the early 1950s. A Saloon (shown) and a Drophead Coupé (*see* 1948) were offered. After a few cars had been produced the company was taken

12B Jowett Javelin

12C Lagonda 2½-Litre

over by David Brown. At the time this was claimed to be Britain's only production car with independent front and rear suspension. Early production had a Cotal four-speed electro-magnetic epicyclic gearbox. This became an extra-cost option when a David Brown synchro-mesh gearbox was made standard equipment.

A Most Unusual 'Ten'

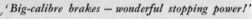

LAN 1947

'Big-calibre brakes — wonderful stopping power!'

Why is it that even when you brake harshly, and your Lanchester pulls up dead, there is none of that catapult feeling? It is because the brake torque reaction is entirely absorbed by the patented Daimler independent front wheel suspension. This completely damps out the usual pitch forward of sudden braking. The Lanchester's brakes are not only very sure — they are also very smooth. The Lanchester 'Ten' is a fast car. You need really good brakes. You've got them!

LANCHESTER 'TEN' with the Daimler Fluid Transmission

13A Lanchester Ten

The New 14 h.p. Two-Door, Fixed-Head Coupé

13C Lea-Francis 14 HP

13A: **Lanchester** offered only one model, the Ten Saloon, Series LD10. It was a four-door six-light car with sliding roof and preselector gearbox (with fluid flywheel) as standard equipment. The car was in production from early 1946 until 1949 (q.v.). The engine was a 1287-cc (63·5 × 101·6 mm) OHV Four with Zenith carburettor and a maximum power output of 40 bhp. Price £927 (chassis £530 basic).

13B: **Lea-Francis** offered Twelve and Fourteen Saloon models on 9 ft 3 in wheelbase chassis with leaf-sprung rigid axles. 1946 Saloons had a 'double waistline'. For 1947 the side windows were enlarged and the upper waistline eliminated. The Fourteen was available with estate car (Utility) bodywork and in October 1947, 1½-Litre and Fourteen 2/4-seater Sports models were introduced, the former using a twin-carb. 64-bhp edition of the 50-bhp Twelve engine.

13C: **Lea-Francis** produced a small series of these Coupé models on their 14 HP chassis. These featured, as standard equipment, a radio, heater, combined electric clock and mirror, twin electric fuel pumps and Dunlopillo upholstery. To the 'foreign' reader it may be of interest to know that the usual British nomenclature for coupés is as follows: Fixed-Head Coupé (Coupé), Drop-Head or Drophead Coupé (Convertible Coupé) and Pillarless Coupé (Hardtop Coupé).

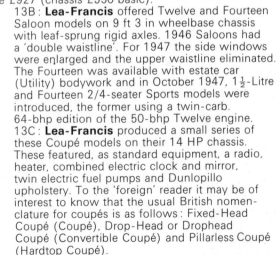

13B Lea-Francis 12 & 14 HP

1947

14A MG Midget TC

14A: **MG** TC was in production from November 1945, until December 1949, and was fundamentally the same as the pre-war TB model. The engine was a 1250-cc OHV Four with twin SUs and four-speed gearbox. Wheelbase was 7 ft 10 in, tyre size 4.50-19 on wire-spoke wheels. UK price was £528.

14B MG 1¼-Litre

14B: **MG** 1¼-Litre Y-type, Model YA, was a four-seater four-door £672 Saloon with single-carburettor version of the TC-type engine (XPAG), independent front suspension, rack-and-pinion steering, and disc wheels. A very attractive car, it was produced until 1951, when it was superseded by the slightly modified Model YB.

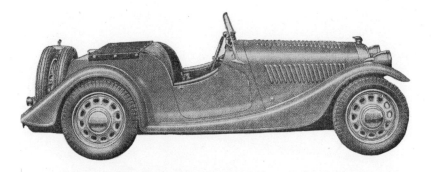

15B Morris Eight

15C Morris Ten

15A: **Morgan** four-wheeled models were fundamentally the same as in the late 1930s, although the engine had been changed from the Ford Ten to a 1267-cc OHV Four, specially made for Morgans by the Standard Motor Co. Shown are the Two-seater, Four-Seater and Coupé in their early form. The underslung chassis frame was interesting in having side members of deep 'Z' section, the floor boards being carried on the lower and the bodywork bolted to the top edges. Front suspension was independent and of the well-known Morgan system, with coil-sprung sliding stub axle carriers.

15B: **Morris** Eight, Series E, four-door Saloon was continued virtually unchanged from 1946. It had a 918-cc 33-bhp OHV Four engine, 7 ft 5 in wheelbase and 4.50-17 tyres. In late 1948 it was superseded by the entirely new Minor, Series MM.

15C: **Morris** Ten, Series M, was substantially the same as in 1946 but featured a restyled curved radiator grille, replacing the earlier flat pattern. The Ten had an 1140-cc 40-bhp OHV four-cylinder engine and 7 ft 6 in wheelbase.

15A Morgan 4/4

1947

1947

16A Nuffield 'Gutty'

16C Oxford Taxicab

16B Nuffield 'Gutty'

16A/B: **Nuffield** 'Gutty' was one of the prototypes of the post-war British military field car or FV1800 Series ¼-ton 4×4 Combat Truck. Later prototypes ('Mudlark') were produced by Nuffield's Wolseley division (*see* 1949). Work on this project had commenced during the war, under direction of Mr Alec Issigonis. The 'Gutty' was powered by a horizontally-opposed four-cylinder engine, similar to that which was planned for the Morris Mosquito (the later Morris Minor), but in both cases the production versions which appeared a few years later had more conventional four-in-line engines.

16C: **Oxford** Taxicab, another Nuffield product, design and series production of which was carried out by Wolseley Motors Ltd at Ward End, Birmingham, was a purpose-built 'hackney carriage' with a wheelbase of 8 ft 11½ in, an overall length of 13 ft 11½ in, and a turning circle of 25 ft. The engine was an 1802·5-cc (75 × 102 mm) OHV Four with dry-sump lubrication, driving through a four-speed gearbox and underslung worm drive rear axle. The artillery type wheels were shod with Dunlop 5.50-18 Super Taxi tyres. The 'cab' was in production during 1947–53 and cost £997 8s. 4d. incl PT.

17A Riley 2½-Litre

THE BEST CAR IN THE WORLD

17B Rolls-Royce Silver Wraith

17A: **Riley** 2½-Litre RMB Saloon was a longer edition of the 1½-Litre RMA which had been introduced in September 1945. The 2½-Litre was added in October 1946, and discontinued in 1953. Engine and transmission were based on the pre-war Riley Sixteen, but the chassis was entirely new and featured Torsionic IFS with torsion bars. The body was of composite construction and was the same as that of the 1½-Litre, with the 'fabric'-covered roof (which, unlike most modern applications, was padded over a fine steel mesh). Main differences between the two cars were the 2½-Litre's light blue (*v.* dark blue) radiator badge and greater length (wheelbase 9 ft 11 in *v.* 9 ft 4½ in, overall length 15 ft 6 in *v.* 14 ft 11 in).

17B: **Rolls-Royce** offered one chassis, the 10 ft 7 in wheelbase 4¼-Litre Silver Wraith. It was available at £2035 (basic) but could be supplied with a variety of catalogued body styles at total prices of up to £6068. Alternatively one could have other coachwork fitted, in which case the PT was calculated on the price of the completed car. The engine was basically the same as that of the Bentley (*q.v.*), but instead of the Bentley's twin SU carburettors, the Rolls-Royce had a single twin-choke Stromberg. Power output, although not advertised, was around the 125 bhp mark.

1947

18A Rover Twelve

18A: **Rover** produced a small quantity of four/five-seater Sports Tourers on their 9 ft 4 in wheelbase Twelve chassis. It would appear that most of these cars were sold overseas in 1947/48, and that some were fitted with the 1389-cc (66·5 × 100 mm) Rover Ten engines. The Twelve had basically the same OHV engine as the Ten, but with 69-mm bore, giving 1496-cc cubic capacity.

18B: **Rover** range comprised Ten, Twelve, Fourteen and Sixteen Saloon models, all with the same basic styling but differing in size of engine, wheelbase, etc. These cars were produced from October 1945 until early 1948. Illustrated is the Sixteen Saloon, which had a 2147-cc (67·5 × 100 mm) four-cylinder OHV engine and 9 ft 7 in wheelbase. Except for engine bore the Fourteen and the Sixteen were very similar.

18C: **Rover** Sixteen was available as Saloon (*see* 18B) and Sports Saloon. The latter is shown here and differed in having 3-in lower four-light bodywork. This alternative styling was also available for the Twelve and Fourteen. The prices, in the case of the Sixteen, were £942 and £964 respectively.

18B Rover Sixteen

18C Rover Sixteen

19A Rover Twelve

19C Rover/Willys

19B Rover Twelve

19A/B: **Rover** Twelve Sports Tourer, shown with boot and roof cover lid open and closed. (*see* also 18A).

19C/D: **Rover**, in 1947, re-engined and re-bodied a war-surplus American Willys 'Jeep' which, after further development, became known as the Land-Rover. The proto-type shown, powered by a Rover four-cylinder OHV engine, was unusual in having the steering wheel, pedals, etc. in a central position, in the fashion of an agricultural tractor. Windscreen, hoodsticks, and many other components were standard or modified 'Jeep' units. Production models (from 1948, *q.v.*) had right- or left-hand drive, doors, and numerous other modifications. Just visible in Fig. 19D is the tubular cross member under the radiator which distin-guished the Willys MB from the Ford-produced GPW 'Jeep' and, in Fig. 19C, the car is shown with an original amphibious 'Jeep'-trailer which, like an early Land-Rover, is now a hard-to-find collector's item. (For a detailed pictorial and factual history of the war-time 'Jeep' the reader is referred to *The Jeep* in this series.)

19D Rover/Willys

1947

20A Singer Nine

20A: **Singer** Nine Roadster sold at £512 and many were exported. It was a full four-seater, designed on traditional lines. The 35-bhp 1074-cc OHC Four drove through a three-speed gearbox (four-speed on 1949–51 models) and was good for 65 mph, returning about 30 mpg. The chassis was basically similar to Singer Motors' other 1947 offerings, the Super Ten and Super Twelve Saloons.

20B: **Singer** Super Twelve was an enlarged edition of the Super Ten, differing mainly in engine size (43-bhp 1525-cc v. 37-bhp 1193-cc, both OHC Fours) and wheelbase (8 ft 7 in v. 7 ft 11 in). Unlike the Ten, the Twelve had a built-out luggage boot, which was its main external distinguishing feature.

20C: **Standard** Eight, Series 48A, was available with three body styles, viz. two-door Saloon with sliding roof and Tourer both at £390, and Drophead Coupé at £410. Illustrated is the Tourer with top erected but without sidescreens. They were carryovers from 1946 and continued until 1948. Engine was a 28-bhp 1009-cc side-valve Four, gearbox four-speed, wheelbase 6 ft 11 in and tyre size 4.75-16.

Introducing
the 'SUPER-TWELVE'

The Singer Super-Twelve, latest of the Singer post-war range, is now in production. A full five-seater, with generous luggage room in the boot, this is a small car only in tax and running costs. In comfort and finish, performance and workmanship, the new Twelve exemplifies the Singer policy which produced the post-war Nine and Ten. A car above and ahead of to-day's accepted standards.

SINGER **M**OTORS

SINGER MOTORS LTD · BIRMINGHAM AND COVENTRY

20B Singer Super Twelve

20C Standard Eight

21A: **Standard** Twelve, Series 12CD, and Fourteen, Series ED, were available as four-door Saloon with sliding roof and as Drophead Coupé. Mechanically the Twelve and Fourteen were similar, with the exception of the cylinder bore which was 69·5 and 73 mm respectively, giving swept volumes of 1609 and 1766 cc. Both were side-valve Fours with Solex carburettor, and maximum output was 44 and 49 bhp. Wheelbase was 8 ft 4 in, tyre size 5.50-16. The same Drophead Coupé, although in scaled-down form, was available on the Eight chassis. These were the last Flying Standards (*see also* 1948).

21B Standard Twelve/Fourteen

21A Standard Twelve

21B: **Standard** Twelve/Fourteen Saloon bodies on their way from the body plant to the final assembly lines at Canley, Coventry. The semi-trailer's tractive unit is a 1946 Bedford-Scammell OSS.

1947

22A Sunbeam-Talbot Ten

22B Sunbeam-Talbot Ten

22A: **Sunbeam-Talbot** Ltd, a division of the Rootes Group, offered two ranges of cars, the Ten and the 2-Litre, both with four-door Saloon (Ten shown), Drophead Coupé and Tourer bodywork. The Ten had an 1185-cc 41-bhp engine, developed from Rootes' popular Hillman Minx side-valve Four, driving through a four-speed gearbox. The wheelbase was 7 ft 10 in, the tyre size 5.25-16. The Saloon had a sliding roof as standard and cost £735.

22B: **Sunbeam-Talbot** Ten with Tourer bodywork cost £697. Mechanically it was similar to the Saloon. The chassis was underslung at the rear and had rigid axles with longitudinal semi-elliptic leaf springs. The Ten Drophead Coupé cost £780.

23A Sunbeam-Talbot 2-Litre

THE TRIUMPH

"1800" SALOON

Manufactured by THE STANDARD MOTOR CO. LTD., COVENTRY

TRIUMPH CARS · FERGUSON TRACTORS · STANDARD CARS

23B Triumph 1800

23A: **Sunbeam-Talbot** 2-Litre Drophead Coupé sold at £895 and was also available as Saloon (£850) and Tourer (£812), all looking similar to the corresponding Ten models (*q.v.*). The 2-Litre models had a 3½-in longer wheelbase than the Tens, and a 1944-cc 56-bhp side-valve four-cylinder engine (the same as the Humber Hawk).
23B: **Triumph** offered two models which were mechanically similar but had totally different bodywork. They were the Series 18T 1800 Saloon (shown) and the Series 18TR 1800 Roadster (*see* 1948). Both were introduced in 1946, after the forming of the Triumph Motor Co. (1945) Ltd by the Standard Motor Co. The Saloon had a wheelbase of 9 ft, the Roadster 8 ft 4 in. The engine was a 65-bhp OHV Four of 1776-cc cubic capacity (bore and stroke 73 × 106 mm). Both models carried a price tag of £991 and, like many others depicted in this book, are now eagerly sought after as collectors' cars.

24A Vauxhall Twelve

24B Vauxhall Fourteen

24D Wolseley Eighteen

24C Wolseley Eight

24A: Vauxhall Twelve, Series HIX, Saloon was produced from March 1946, until July 1948. It had four-light bodywork, like the Ten to which it was similar in appearance and dimensions. The Twelve had a 1442-cc (69·5 × 95 mm) OHV Four engine, producing 35 bhp, with three-speed gearbox. The Ten had a smaller bore (63·5 mm) and an output of 31·5 bhp. Both had Dubonnet type IFS, 8 ft 1¾ in wheelbase and 5.00-16 tyres. The price was also the same, at £422.

24B: Vauxhall Fourteen, Series JIB, was a six-light five/six-seater Saloon with six-cylinder engine of 1781-cc (61·5 × 100 mm), 8 ft 9 in wheelbase and 5.50-16 tyres. It had a built-out luggage boot and carried the spare wheel inside. The steering column was adjustable for length and the price was £557. The specimen shown served as a staff car in the RAF and featured less brightwork than the civilian version.

24C: Wolseley offered Eight (shown), Ten, Twelve (12/48), Fourteen (14/60) and Eighteen (18/85) Saloons, priced from £461 up to £755, and in August announced the Twenty-five (a large Limousine, supplied mainly for official Government use). Eight, Ten and Twelve had four-cylinder engines, the larger models were Sixes, all of different cubic capacities and with overhead valves, SU carburettors (twins on the Sixes) and four-speed gearboxes. Body styling was fundamentally the same throughout the range, featuring the classic Wolseley radiator grille with illuminated badge.

24D: Wolseley Eighteen or 18/85 was in production from late 1945 until December 1948. It had a 2321-cc 85-bhp OHV Six engine and, like the Fourteen, a wheelbase size of 8 ft 8½ in. A sliding roof was optional.

1948

During 1948 many new models were introduced. These were the real post-war designs with new modern full-width body-work and usually with such features as independent front suspension, steering column gear change, bench-type front seats, etc. Most of them were not available for the home market where buyers had to be content with earlier models. These, however, were gradually phased out of production because manufacturers needed all their production capacity for the new models, and owing to a drastic change in the road tax system (a flat rate, rather than based on the old hypothetical RAC formula) there was no longer such a need for the old-fashioned small-bore Eights and Tens. Rationalization and concentration on a minimum number of different models were of paramount importance. Some 330,000 cars were produced, more than two-thirds of which were exported. Home registrations numbered 112,666 new cars and just over 10,000 'hackneys'. 221 cars were imported. New car prices, where quoted, were valid in May 1945, and include purchase tax, unless stated otherwise.

One of the biggest events of 1948 was the first post-war London Motor Show at Earls Court, in October/November. It was the first since 1939, and most manufacturers displayed their new models, the majority of which are considered 1949 models and are shown in the following section.

25B Alvis Fourteen

25A AC 2-Litre

25A : **AC** continued their 2-Litre model, mainly in two-door Saloon form. Illustrated is a rare and rather ungainly 'shooting brake', built on the same chassis. Similar bodies appeared on other high-grade chassis, including Alvis and Riley. When equipped with rear doors and folding rear seat, like this example, they were classed as Utility Cars.

25B : **Alvis** Fourteen, Model TA14, Drophead Coupé was introduced in January 1948, and offered until September of the following year. The bodywork was by Carbodies Ltd, whose plant was opposite Alvis' own, in Coventry's Holyhead Road. The chassis price was £665 (basic), while the complete car cost £1276, which was the same price as for the Saloon.

1948

26A Armstrong Siddeley Hurricane

26B Aston Martin

26C Aston Martin 2-Litre Sports

26A: **Armstrong Siddeley** continued their 1947 Sixteen 2-Litre programme (*q.v.*), comprising the Typhoon two-door and Lancaster four-door Saloons and the Hurricane Drophead Coupé, an example of which is illustrated. It cost £1247. The Typhoon, which was also known as Sportsman's Saloon, carried the same price tag. All three were superseded, in September 1949, by 2309-cc engined models.

26B: **Aston Martin** and Lagonda (*q.v.*) were taken over in 1947 by David Brown (later Sir David). At this time the tubular chassis and a new 1970-cc OHV engine were still under development. Shown is the first DB Aston Martin, the car that won the Spa 24-hour race in 1948. The picture shows the car as it was at the 1948 London Motor Show,

with revised bodywork. A similar car, called the Spa Replica, was marketed during 1948/49 at £3110.

26C: **Aston Martin** 2-Litre Sports 2-4-seater was the first post-war Aston Martin to be offered to the public, at £2332 (October 1948). The prototype had run as a practice car at Spa. The 1970-cc (82·55 × 92 mm) four-cylinder pushrod OHV engine had a CR of 7·25:1 and twin SU carburettors. The maximum power output was 90 bhp at 4750 rpm (95 bhp on the Spa Replica model). Both cars had a four-speed gearbox and 9 ft wheelbase. The Sports (later known as DB1) had 5.75-16 tyres, the Spa Replica 5,25-18, both on wire spoke wheels. They were produced at Feltham in Middlesex.

27A: **Austin** 1946/47 models were discontinued with the exception of the Sixteen Model BS1 Saloon and BW1 Countryman. This somewhat 'customized' saloon was photographed in the late 1960s.

27A Austin Sixteen

27B Austin A40 Dorset

In keeping with the finest traditions of British craftsmanship yet modern in every flowing line and refinement of comfort. The Vanden Plas PRINCESS ON THE AUSTIN 135 CHASSIS

27C Austin A135 Princess

27B: **Austin** A40 two-door Dorset, Model G2S2, and four-door Devon, Model GS2, Saloons superseded the earlier Eight, Ten and Twelve in October 1947, at £403 and £416 respectively. The Dorset was phased out during 1948. They had a 1200-cc (65·48 × 89 mm) 40-bhp (10·7 HP) OHV Four engine with four-speed gearbox, IFS with coil springs and Girling hydro-mechanical brakes. Wheelbase was 7 ft 8½ in and tyre size 5.00-16. In March 1948, a 10-cwt Van (GV2) derivative was added, followed by Countryman (GP2) and Pick-up (GQU2) modifications thereof in September.

27C: **Austin** A135 Princess, Model DS2, was mechanically similar to the A125 Sheerline, Model DS1, except for triple SU carburettors (v. single Stromberg) and higher final drive ratio. The main difference was that the £1277 Sheerline was entirely Austin-built, whereas the £2103 Princess had coachwork by Vanden Plas. Both had a 4-litre OHV Six engine and coil-spring IFS. Successors to a long line of Austin Twenties, the A125 and A135 were continued for many years in various forms, including limousines and ambulances.

28: **Austin** A40s were sold in considerable numbers all around the world. The first A40 Devon in New York is shown here looking rather forlorn in Fifth Avenue traffic. When eventually discontinued in early 1952, over 344,000 A40s had been produced; 77% of these had been exported, earning £88 million in foreign currency. In February 1950, it was announced that the A40 had been identified as the individual British product that had earned more dollars for Britain than any other one-make commodity, namely $70 million in 160 weeks.

1948

28 Austin A40 Devon (*see* page 27)

29A Bond Minicar

29B Bristol 400

29C Citroën light Fifteen

29A: **Bond** Aircraft and Engineering Co. (Blackpool) Ltd of Longridge, Lancs, introduced their first three-wheeler in mid-1948. Intended as a 'runabout for shopping and calls within a 20—30 mile radius', the car had a chassisless body of stressed-skin construction. It was powered by a 125-cc Villiers two-stroke engine, mounted on a swivelling fork which carried the front wheel, suspension being by means of a trailing link. The brakes operated only on the unsprung but resiliently and independently mounted rear wheels. Shown is a prototype, quantity production commenced in 1949 (Mark A).

29B: **Bristol** 400 2-Litre underwent several changes such as a larger boot and external spare wheel mounting with fitted cover and, as can be seen here, conventional bumpers instead of the tubular type (*see* 1947).

29C: **Citroën** Cars Ltd have been assemblers of Citroën front-wheel drive cars for many years, importing the body pressings and mechanical components from France. Many British-made components and fittings were utilized. The Light Fifteen, Model PVS (shown) was in production for exactly ten years, from October 1945, and in October 1948, was joined by the Series 15C Six which was similar but larger (wb 10 ft 1½ in v. 9 ft 6½ in, 2866-cc six-cylinder engine v. 1911-cc Four, etc.).

1948

30A Commer Superpoise

COACHWORK DE LUXE by TICKFORD

DAIMLER TICKFORD D.H. COUPE
LONDON SHOWROOMS:
TICKFORD LTD. 6-9 UPPER SAINT MARTIN'S LANE, LONDON W.C.2
WORKS: NEWPORT PAGNELL · BUCKS.

30B Daimler 2½-Litre

30A: **Commer** Superpoise passenger-utility vehicle, based on light truck chassis. It was supplied to Vickers-Armstrongs Ltd, Supermarine Works. It was powered by what was basically the same 1944-cc four-cylinder engine as that used in the contemporary Humber Hawk, both makes being members of the Rootes Group.

30B: **Daimler** continued their 2½-Litre DB18 in Saloon and Drophead Coupé form. The chassis was available at a basic price of £1065 for bodywork by other coachbuilders and shown here is a Drophead Coupé by Tickford Ltd of Newport Pagnell, Bucks.

31: **Ford** Pilot Saloon, Model E71A, was introduced in August 1947, and continued until 1951. Except for the front end, the four-door four-light bodywork was very similar to that of the pre-war 22 HP Model 62. When the Pilot was introduced there was to be a choice of 2·5- and 3·6-litre V8 engines, but it was soon decided to fit only the larger unit (basically identical to that of the contemporary Fordson Thames trucks). This 3622-cc (77·8 × 95·3 mm) unit produced 85 bhp at 3500 rpm and drove through a three-speed gearbox with steering-column mounted shift lever. Suspension was in the Ford tradition with rigid axles and transverse leaf springs. Available for export was an 'equipped chassis' (Model E71C) for pick-up truck bodies. Some export models had vertical louvres in the bonnet side panels. A metal Estate Car variant was offered, but supplied almost exclusively to Government departments. The Anglia and Prefect were continued with little change except that in December 1947, the word 'Anglia' had been incorporated in the radiator grille badge and the Prefect had chrome radiator slats and plain hub caps from October 1947.

31 Ford Pilot (*see* page 30)

1948

32A Hillman Minx

32B Hillman Minx

32C Hillman Minx

32A: **Hillman** Minx for 1948, announced in December 1947, and known as the Mark II, was facelifted and modified in several respects. Bonnet, bumpers, front wings and dashboard were restyled and the four-speed gearbox had steering-column gearshift. The radiator grille was no longer integral with the bonnet and the headlamps were built-in. The wheels were now of the full-disc type. Another important modification was the change from mechanical to hydraulic brakes. The Saloon was priced at £493.

32B: **Hillman** Minx Mark II Drophead Coupé featured the same improvements and modifications as the Mark II Saloon (q.v.), plus the omission of the 'hood irons' of the convertible top. The Mark II Minxes were not produced for very long. After nine months they were superseded by the entirely restyled Mark III models (see 1949).

32C: **Hillman** Minx Mark II Estate Car shared its rear body styling with the Minx-derived Commer light van.

33A HRG

33C Humber Pullman

33B Humber Hawk

33A: **HRG** 1100 and 1500 sports two-seaters with their characteristic quarter-elliptic leaf-sprung tubular front axle were continued from 1947 (*q.v.*) but production of the 90-mph Aerodynamic model was dropped. The 1100 and 1500 were continued until the mid-1950s when all HRG production ceased. Shown is one of several preserved HRGs attending a rally in England in the early 1970s.

33B: **Humber** Hawk, Snipe and Super Snipe were continued from 1947 with very little change except the adoption of steering-column gearshift on the Hawk, in September 1947, the chassis of which is shown. The system was called 'Synchromatic finger-tip gear change'. With this modification the Hawk was now known as Mark II but all three cars were discontinued in September/October and superseded in production by the entirely newly-styled Hawk Mark III and face-lifted Super Snipe Mark II (*see* 1949).

33C: **Humber** Pullman was the first Humber to receive a post-war face-lift, clearly from the same Rootes stylists responsible for the Hillman Minx Mark II (*q.v.*). The Pullman in its basic form was a Limousine and the new edition, again bodied by Thrupp & Maberley, was designated Mark II. Illustrated are two special-bodied Pullmans, produced for the Royal Tour of Australia and New Zealand. Humber, in conjunction with the Governments concerned, provided three Landaulettes (*right*) and two Touring Cabriolets (*left*) for Australia, and two Landaulettes for New Zealand. In addition ten standard Pullman Limousines and nine Super Snipes were supplied for the two Tours.

1948

34A Invicta Black Prince

34B Invicta Black Prince

34C Jaguar 3½-Litre

34A/B: Invicta Black Prince Byfleet Drophead Coupé was produced in 1948 and was priced at £3890. It superseded the Wentworth Saloon which was still available to special order, but which was produced mainly in 1947. Both were made only in small numbers and had many unconventional design features such as a Brockhouse Turbo Torque Converter transmission giving infinitely variable gear ratios (plus epicyclic reversing gear), X-form frame with torsion bar independent springing front and rear, inboard rear brakes, etc. The 2998-cc 120-bhp six-cylinder engine embodied a 24-volt dynamotor, coupled direct to the front end of the crankshaft. The power unit was based on a Meadows industrial engine and had twin overhead camshafts, non-adjustable valves and three SU carburettors. The coachwork was made by Jensen of West Bromwich

34C: Jaguar 1½-, 2½- and 3½-Litre Saloon models were continued from 1947 (*q.v.*) and in October were joined by revised 2½- and 3½-Litre Mark V models (*see* 1949). Mid-1948 prices were: 1½-Litre £953 (special equipment model £1009), 2½-Litre £1189, 3½-Litre £1263. Note the very long radio aerial on this Swiss-registered car.

35A Jowett Javelin

35B Lagonda 2½-Litre

35A: **Jowett** continued their successful Javelin and 'owing to popular demand from overseas' introduced a Drophead Coupé variant: a five-seater with a three-abreast bench seat plus a separate two-seat 'dickey' in the rear (outside). It was displayed at the 1948 Earls Court Motor Show. The tail end of necessity being unusually long, this car looked very ill-proportioned and, not surprisingly, was not produced in quantity. The attractive front end of the Javelin is shown (*see also* 1947).

35B: **Lagonda** 2½-Litre Saloon and Drophead Coupé (shown) were produced in very small quantity in 1946/47, after which the company was bought by Mr David Brown who resumed production by the autumn of 1948. The 2580-cc (78 × 90 mm) engine had twin overhead camshafts and twin SU carburettors. It developed 105 bhp at 5000 rpm. Wheelbase was 9 ft 5½ in. Suspension was independent with coil springs at front and torsion bars at rear. Prices in August 1948: Saloon £3110, Drophead Coupé £3421.

1948

36A : **Lea-Francis** Cars Ltd of Coventry, in addition to their Fourteen Saloon, Coupé and Utility models, offered this 14 HP 1767-cc Sports Two-seater on 8 ft 3 in wheelbase chassis. On the home market it was priced at £1276. It was also available with a 12 HP 1496-cc engine, at the same price.

36A Lea-Francis 14 HP

36B MG Midget TC

36C MG 1¼-Litre

36B : **MG** Midget TC was a carryover from 1947 and continued to sell well, especially in North America. It was particularly popular in California, where it created much goodwill for British sports cars. The car had a top speed of 75 mph and was used on both street and track. In Britain the price was £528 throughout its production span.
36C : **MG** 1¼-Litre Saloon, designated Model YA, continued to sell at £672. Including its slightly modified successor (the 1951–53 YB) and the YT Tourer version, which had twin carburettors (1948–50), an overall total of about 8700 were produced.

1948

37A: **Morgan** Three-Wheelers lined up at a British rally attracting all kinds of veteran, vintage and other special-interest vehicles in the early 1970s. Right to left: 1948, 1935 and 1949 Morgans. Four-wheeled models for 1948 were continued from 1947 (*q.v.*)

37B: **Morris** Eight, Series E, four-door Saloon 'ghost view'. This car was in production from 1939 until November 1948. During its last year it had a spring-type steering wheel. In addition to the two- and four-door car models there was a 5-cwt Van variant, Series Z, which was continued until May 1953.

37C: **Morris** Ten, Series M, was a carryover from previous years and was replaced in October 1948, by the all-new Morris Oxford, Series MO (*see 1949*).

THE MORRIS EIGHT (Series "E")

37B Morris Eight

37A Morgan Three-Wheelers

37C Morris Ten

1948

38A Renault Eight

38B Riley 2½-Litre

38A: **Renault** Eight, Model BFK4, as shown here, was assembled during 1947–50 by Renault Ltd of Western Avenue, Acton, London W3, largely from components imported from France and mainly for export. Although this 1948 advertisement claims that it was a genuine post-war car, it was in fact a continuation of the pre-war Juvaquatre (Eight in the UK), but with four doors and hydraulic brakes. As in 1939, the engine was a 1003-cc (58 × 95 mm) side-valve Four, driving through a three-speed gearbox. Front suspension was independent with a transversal leaf spring, wheelbase was 7 ft 8½ in, tyre size 4.75-16. In 1949/50 it was superseded by the rear-engined Renault 4CV (750), although the van variant (AHG2) was continued in France until 1953.

38B: **Riley** 1½- and 2½-Litre RMA and RMB Saloons were continued from 1947 (*q.v.*) with only minor technical changes. The 2½-Litre, for example, was fitted with larger inlet valves from April and two leading shoe front brakes from June. From July interior bonnet locks were fitted. Price was £1125 (£863 for the 1½-Litre).

38C: **Riley** introduced this three-seater RMC Roadster in March 1948, on the 9 ft 11 in wheelbase 2½-Litre chassis. It was originally made only for export, like the Drophead Coupé variant (*see* 1949) which appeared in September 1948. In September of 1949 these two models were made available for the home market. The Roadster was produced until December 1950, after it had been changed to a two-seater in January of that year.

38C Riley 2½-Litre

39A: **Rolls-Royce** Silver Wraith $4\frac{1}{4}$-Litre chassis, illustrated with Sedanca DeVille coachwork by H. J. Mulliner & Co. Ltd. This was one of several body styles available. The price of the complete car was £6029 (*see also* 1947).

39B: **Rover**, in February 1948, replaced their previous range of 10, 12, 14 and 16 HP cars by two new models, designated the P3 Series. There were two basic models, the Sixty with four-cylinder and the Seventy-Five with six-cylinder engine. The two cars shared the same 9 ft $2\frac{1}{2}$ in wheelbase chassis, with minor differences to front suspension and gearbox. The difference in engine length was made up by an elongated bell-housing in the case of the shorter Sixty engine.

39C: **Rover** P3 Series models, both in four-cylinder Sixty and six-cylinder Seventy-Five form, were available with either four- or six-light (shown) four-door body styles, without price difference, i.e. both Sixties sold at £1080, both Seventy-Fives at £1106. Compared with the previous Rover Twelve, the external differences were mainly in the bumpers, horns, fog lamp position and rear lamps. They were also shorter and wider. The engines were entirely new and featured overhead inlet and side exhaust valves (F-head). Cubic capacities were 1595-cc (69·5 × 105 mm) and 2103 cc (65·2 × 105 mm) for the Four and the Six respectively.

39B Rover, Sixty and Seventy-Five

39A Rolls-Royce Silver Wraith

39C Rover Sixty and Seventy-Five

1948

40A: **Rover's** new four-wheel drive utility
vehicle, very appropriately called Land-Rover
(one of the cleverest features of the vehicle!),
went into quantity production in July 1948,
after having made its world début at the
Amsterdam Motor Show in April. The first
model is shown here alongside a Series III
Regular version of 25 years and about 850,000
vehicles later. The first Land-Rovers had
the same engine as the Rover Sixty car (*q.v.*).
40B: **Singer** Nine Roadster and Super Ten and
Twelve Saloons were continued from 1947
(*q.v.*), now at £576, £652 and £768
respectively. Posing on the old 'penny-farthing'
is actor Dirk Bogarde.
40C: **Standard** phased out their old Flying
Eight, Twelve (shown) and Fourteen models in
the summer of 1948, and concentrated on their
entirely new Vanguard Saloon.

40B Singer Super Twelve

40A Rover Land-Rover

40C Standard Twelve

41A Standard Vanguard

41A: **Standard** decided in 1947 to pursue a one-model policy with their new and very attractive Vanguard Saloon, Series 20S. It was a new car from the ground up and went into full-scale quantity production in 1948. Initially, i.e. until the end of the year, practically all Vanguards were exported. The car had IFS, four-cylinder OHV engine (2088 cc; 85×92 mm; 68 bhp at 4000 rpm), three-speed gearbox, with right-hand column shift, 7 ft 10 in wheelbase, 13 ft 10 in overall length, 5 ft 9 in overall width (providing accommodation for up to six passengers) and 5.50-16 tyres. In October an Estate Car variant was introduced, followed by a Van and later a Pick-up truck. Basically the same engine was used in the Ferguson tractor.

41B: **Sunbeam-Talbot** Ten was continued from 1947 (*q.v.*), in Saloon, Drophead Coupé (shown) and Tourer form, until mid-1948 when the entirely new 80 models appeared (*see* 1949).

41C: **Sunbeam-Talbot** 2-Litre, which was similar but somewhat larger than the Ten, was also continued from 1947 (*q.v.*) and superseded in June by the new 90. The Tourer versions were discontinued.

41B Sunbeam-Talbot Ten

41C Sunbeam-Talbot 2-Litre

1948

42 Triumph 1800 Roadster

42 : **Triumph** continued their 1800 Saloon, Series 18T (*see* 1947) and 1800 Roadster, Series 18TR (shown), with virtually no changes until October when the Roadster was fitted with the same 2088-cc engine and three-speed gearbox as the Standard Vanguard. It was redesignated the 2000 Roadster, Series 20TR. The same change was made to the 1800 Saloon in February 1949.

43A/B : **Vauxhall** Motors kept their 1946–47 Twelve and Fourteen Saloons in production until July, when they were superseded by the restyled Wyvern and Velox models (*see* 1949). Illustrated is the Model HIX Twelve Saloon.

43C : **Wolseley** Twelve (12/48), Series III, another example of a basically pre-war car which was in its last production year. In October it was superseded by a new model, the Four-fifty (*see* 1949). The Wolseley Eight, Ten, Fourteen (14/60), Eighteen (18/85) and Twenty-five were also phased out during the year.

43A Vauxhall Twelve

43B Vauxhall Twelve

43C Wolseley Twelve

1949

By 1949 practically all British production cars were of new post-war design and most of them had been drastically redesigned or at least restyled. All were shown at the first post-war Earls Court Motor Show in London in late 1948, which needless to say, drew record crowds. Production during 1949 soared to an all-time high of 412,920 cars and 216,373 commercial vehicles, representing weekly averages of 7929 and 4161 respectively. Of the new cars 257,250 were exported, valued at just over £72½ million. 1868 cars were imported, worth just over half a million pounds. New car registrations at home were up by almost 40 per cent. Of the 1949 cars the Editor of 'The Motor' wrote: 'At last our new cars are ready . . . In the most competitive markets in the world Britain can now claim the fastest, the finest, and the best finished automobiles available to the motoring public. In the vital matters of economy of operation, road holding, acceleration and braking, we can collectively or individually more than hold our own'.

44B Allard P1

44A AC 2-Litre

44A: **AC** 2-Litre Drophead Coupé was introduced in March 1949, and was in production for only a very short period. It was discontinued in 1950 after only about twenty had been made, most of which went for export. AC's principal product was the two-door Saloon (*see* 1947).
44B: **Allard** P1 two-door Saloon first appeared in 1949 and was continued until 1953. It was basically similar to the open cars which had been in production since 1946, powered by Ford V8 engines and using many other Ford components. The P1 had an aluminium panelled coachbuilt body and sold at £1277.
44C: **Alvis** Fourteen, Model TA14, was offered in chassis, Saloon (shown) and Drophead Coupé form. The latter was discontinued in September 1949, the Saloon in October of the following year.

44C Alvis Fourteen TA14

45C : **Aston Martin** 2-Litre Sports of 1948/49 became known as the DB1 with the advent of the DB2 (*q.v.*). Front suspension was independent with trailing arms, coil springs and anti-roll torsion bar. The rear axle was rigid, with coil springs, the torque being taken by arms extending from the axle to a cross member of the square-section fabricated steel tube frame.

45D : **Aston Martin** DB2 prototype, which was third at Spa in 1949 and raced at Le Mans in 1949 and 1950. This car was a development of Claude Hill's tubular space frame chassis with Tickford two-seater coupé bodywork. It was fitted with the 2·6-litre engine designed by W. O. Bentley for Lagonda (which, like Aston Martin and Tickford, was acquired by David Brown).

45A Alvis Fourteen TB14

45B Alvis Fourteen TB14

45C Aston Martin DB1

45D Aston Martin DB2

45A/B : **Alvis** Fourteen, Model TB14, Special Sports Tourer was introduced in October 1948. The bodywork was reportedly designed in Belgium and not surprisingly was frowned upon by traditional Alvis customers. Underneath was a 9 ft wheelbase modified Fourteen chassis with a twin-carburettor 68-bhp variant of the standard 1892-cc OHV Four engine.

1949

AUSTINS LAST LONGER

46A Austin A40 Devon

46A : **Austin** Motor Company's bread-and-butter model was the A40 Devon four-door Saloon, a carryover from 1948 (*q.v.*).

46B : **Austin** A70 Hampshire Saloon, Model BS2, was introduced in July 1948, and had the same 2199-cc engine as the old Sixteen (which was discontinued in March 1949). The Hampshire was produced until early 1951 and could be called a scaled-up edition of the A40 Devon. It featured IFS and steering-column gearshift. Brakes were Girling hydraulic 2LS front, mechanical rear and wheelbase was 8 ft. From November an Estate Car version was offered, the Model BW3 Countryman.

46C : **Austin** A90 Atlantic Convertible, Model DB2, appeared in February 1949. It featured rather unusual body styling and was powered by a twin-carburettor (SU) 2660-cc OHV Four engine of 88 bhp (a larger-bore edition of the Sixteen and A70 engine). The Atlantic made history at Indianapolis, USA, where it broke many international records during an impressive run which lasted seven days and nights.

46D : **Austin** A125 Sheerline DS1 (shown) and A135 Princess DS2 (*see* 1948) were carryovers from the previous year. In September 1949, an A125 Limousine was introduced. This car, designated Model DM1, was a lengthened six-light edition of the Saloon, with a wheelbase of 11 ft (*v.* 9 ft 11½ in). It had a glass partition between front and rear compartment and a two-piece propeller shaft. A Touring Limousine (DM2) version of the Vanden Plas bodied A135 Princess had been introduced in the previous October.

46C Austin A90 Atlantic

46B Austin A70 Hampshire

46D Austin A125 Sheerline

47A : Austin Hire Car, Model FL1, was a four-door edition of the FX3 Taxi (1948–59) with single-piece front seat. It had the 2·2-litre (2199-cc) OHV Four engine, developing 67 bhp at 3800 rpm, driving through a four-speed gearbox and underslung worm drive rear axle. Brakes were Girling mechanical and four hand-operated Smith hydraulic jacks were standard fitments. Turning circle was 35 ft. Later models had a hypoid-type rear axle.

47B : Bentley models from September 1948, featured a narrow chromium waistline strip, curved rear wing valances (half-spats) and new type pleated upholstery. As usual, there was a selection of body styles to choose from, including several by well-known coachbuilders. Shown is the Four-door Sports Saloon as produced by the makers, Bentley Motors (1931) Ltd, themselves and costing £4038. It was generally known as the 'standard body'.

47C : Bristol produced three types of cars, namely the 400 (*see* 1948), the 401 (five-seater Saloon, from September 1948) and the 402 (Convertible version of 401). The latter chassis was used also by some other coachbuilders, including Pinin Farina (later Pininfarina) of Turin, Italy. Shown is a Farina *Cabriolet 2 posti*.

47B Bentley 4¼-Litre Mark VI

47A Austin Hire Car

47C Bristol 401/402

1949

48A Daimler 2½-Litre DB18

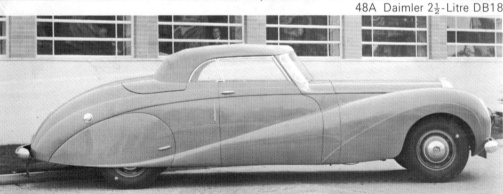

48B Daimler Straight Eight

48C Daimler Straight Eight

48D Daimler Straight Eight

48A: **Daimler** 2½-Litre DB18 Special Sports Coupé, bodied by Barker, was made from October 1948 until 1953. It had a twin-carburettor OHV Six engine with light-alloy cylinder head, producing 85 bhp at 4200 rpm (v. 70 bhp of the standard 2½-Litre). Price was £2560.
48B: **Daimler** Straight Eight, Model DE36, chassis with Drophead Coupé bodywork by Hooper. This huge car, shown at the Earls Court Motor Show in October/November 1948, was finished in canary yellow and cost £7000. The 12 ft 3 in wheelbase chassis sold at the basic price of £2025, the coachwork always being produced and fitted by specialist coachbuilders.

48C/D: **Daimler** Straight Eight with Limousine coachwork by Hooper. The engine was an OHV eight-cylinder in-line 5½-Litre with two SU carburettors and an output of 150 bhp at 3600 rpm. It drove the hypoid rear axle through a fluid flywheel with preselector gearbox. Also available in chassis form only was the DE27, a six-cylinder variant with the same bore and stroke (85·1 × 120 mm) and shorter wheelbase (11 ft 6½ in).

49A Ford Anglia

49B Ford Prefect

49C Ford Pilot

49A: **Ford** Anglia received a facelift in October 1948, and was re-designated Model E494A. The new radiator grille followed the same contour as that of the Eights and Tens of 1937–39, but now had two upright vertically-slatted openings. Introduced at the same time was an Anglia export version with the 1172-cc engine of the Prefect. This car differed in having a '10' radiator badge, the rear number plate mounted on the left and an extra tail lamp. The 1953–59 Ford Popular 103E was a direct descendant from this export-Anglia (which could be bought in the UK only for dollars!). The E494A standard Anglia retained the smaller-bore 933-cc engine. Both were long-stroke (92·5 mm) Fours.
49B: **Ford** Prefect also had a restyled front end, but more so than the Anglia. The radiator grille of the Prefect, now designated E493A, was not unlike that of the larger Pilot (*q.v.*) but the headlamps were incorporated in the wings, which were also higher than before. In its new form, but retaining the old 1172-cc engine, it was made until 1953.
49C: **Ford** Pilot V8, Model E71A, was continued with periodical modifications and improvements, rather than annual face-lifts. In March 1949, for example, the rear axle ratio was changed from 4·11 to 3·78:1, and a bonnet safety catch was added.

D

1949

50A Hillman Minx

50B Hillman Minx

50A/B : **Hillman** Minx models were entirely restyled for the 1949 model year. The new Mark III models, introduced in September 1948, incorporated the most drastic changes in the long line of these popular family cars since 1936 (the original Minx dated back to 1931). The full-width bodywork was styled by Raymond Loewy, who was also responsible for the post-war Studebakers. The new car retained most of the existing mechanical components but had IFS with coil springs. Wheelbase was 7 ft 9 in. Price £505.

50C : **Hillman** Minx Mark III Drophead Coupé shared the 1949 restyling with the Saloon. Compared with the Mark II it now had rear quarter windows, which could be cranked down into the bodysides. The price was £576.

50C Hillman Minx

1949

51A: **Hillman** Minx Estate Car, as before, combined the styling of the Saloon and the Commer Supervan. The Estate Car sold at £595, the Van at £350. They had the same 1185-cc side-valve Four engine as the other Minxes.

51B/C: **Humber** Hawk was completely restyled, along the same lines as Rootes' smaller Hillman Minx, the main difference being the vertical radiator grille. Unlike the Minx, the Hawk retained a separate chassis frame. The new model was designated Mark III and, again like the Hillman Minx, featured IFS, but had the engine of the previous model, in this case the 1944-cc side-valve Four unit (which was also used in certain Rootes Commer and Karrier trucks). Wheelbase was 8 ft 9½ in, price £799.

51B Humber Hawk

51A Hillman Minx

51C Humber Hawk

1949

52A Humber Super Snipe

52A: **Humber** Super Snipe for 1949 (Mark II) was also restyled, but not as dramatically as the Hawk. It was now a full six-seater, with longer wheelbase, steering-column gearshift and other modifications. The engine was basically the same 4086-cc 100-bhp Six as before. The Snipe was discontinued. The Pullman (*see* 1948) became available in Saloon form, without partition and designated Imperial, and the Super Snipe Saloon was joined by a Touring Limousine variant, both in the autumn of 1949.

52B Humber Super Snipe

52B: **Humber** Super Snipe Drophead Coupé was produced in very small quantity by Tickford. The top was of the three-position type: fully open, half closed (shown) and fully closed.

53A/B/C: **Jaguar** Mark V models, Saloon (shown) and Drophead Coupé, were introduced in October 1948. They were available with 2½- and 3½-Litre engine. The 1½-Litre model was discontinued in March 1949, and the old style 2½- and 3½-Litre Saloons (*see* 1948) were kept in production until October.

53A Jaguar Mark V

53B Jaguar Mark V

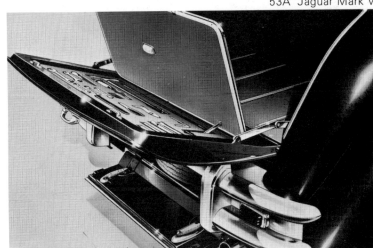

53C Jaguar Mark V

1949

55A Jaguar XK120

55A : **Jaguar** XK120 was uniquely and beautifully styled, based in part on ideas from Piet Olyslager, who was also responsible for the French Lago Talbots and others of the same era. The car was originally intended for a limited production run, but the demand was so great, particularly in the USA, that it was kept in production until 1954 and then continued in XK140 and 150 form until superseded by the E-type in 1961.

55B : **Jaguar** XK120s in standard and modified form took part in numerous sporting events. This picture shows the 1949 Silverstone race winner in full swing, hotly pursued by another XK and a Healey. In 1951 a special competition version appeared : the C-Type (XK120C), which was very successful at Le Mans.

54 : **Jaguar** (XK120, a brand new and sensational Sports Two-Seater, hit the automotive world like a bombshell. It had a new twin-OHC 3½-Litre 160-bhp six-cylinder engine, extremely fast and yet sufficiently docile for ordinary motoring. On a stretch of the Brussels-Ostend motorway near Jabbeke, an XK120 was officially timed at over 132 mph, the only non-standard fitment being an undershield. An American journal, Californian Autonews, wrote : 'it is typically British that Jaguar never claimed more than 120 mph for this car'.

55B Jaguar XK120

1949

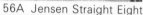
56A Jensen Straight Eight

56C Lagonda 2½-Litre

56B Jowett Javelin

56A: **Jensen** Motors Ltd of West Bromwich, who before the war had built Ford V8-engined Specials, announced a new luxury car in 1946. Actual series production commenced in 1948, there being a four-door Saloon and a four-door Convertible. The eight-cylinder OHV engine, produced by Henry Meadows Ltd, had a capacity of 3860 cc and a maximum output of 130 bhp. In September 1949, this engine was replaced by the 4-litre Six of the Austin A125 Sheerline.

56B: **Jowett** Javelin, Series PA, one of the first of British post-war car designs (*see* 1947) kept selling well at home and overseas. In September, the 1950 Series PB was announced in Standard and De Luxe form, with differences in trim and equipment. Javelins came 1st and 3rd in the 1949 Monte Carlo Rally (1½-litre class) and 1st in the Belgian 24-hour Grand Prix (2-litre touring class).

56C: **Lagonda** 2½-Litre Mark I Saloon was continued from 1948 without change and produced until October 1952. The Mark I Drophead Coupé (*see* 1948) was continued until 1953.

57A Lanchester Ten

57B Lea-Francis Fourteen

57C MG Midget TC

57A: **Lanchester** Ten, Series LD10, with all-steel saloon bodywork by Briggs, was conceived before the war and produced from 1946 until September 1949, when it was replaced by a four-light Barker-bodied (coachbuilt) saloon on the same 8 ft 3 in wheelbase chassis. This is the Briggs-bodied car (*see also* 1947). The Barker-bodied successor was made until mid-1951.

57B: **Lea-Francis** Fourteen for 1949 had restyled six-light bodywork with the head-lamps incorporated in the front end, and front wings flowing back to blend in with the rear wings. The 9 ft 3 in wheelbase chassis now had IFS with torsion bars. There were two versions: the Mark V and Mark VI (shown), the latter being a luxurious edition with sliding roof, heater, radio, etc. Both were made primarily for export.

57C: **MG** Midget TC was now in its last year and for 1950 (TD) was modified in several respects such as the adoption of IFS, rack and pinion steering (as on Y-type) and bolt-on disc wheels. Of the TC approximately 10,000 were built from late 1945 until December 1949.

1949

58A Morris Minor

58C Morris Oxford

58B Morris Minor

58A: **Morris** introduced their completely new post-war designs in October 1948, following many years of development. The development of the Minor, in fact, can be traced back to the war years when Mr (later Sir) Alec Issigonis first put its basic shape on paper. It was then code-named Mosquito and intended to have a flat-four engine. When it appeared as the Minor it was powered by the 918-cc Series E engine of the Eight which it replaced, but apart from this the car was a total departure from earlier Morris practice.

58B: **Morris** Minor, Series MM, was available originally in two-door Saloon and Tourer (shown) variants. Later more body styles were added and, from June 1951, the Tourer was known as Convertible. The Minor had a 27·5-bhp side-valve Four engine with four-speed gearbox and 7 ft 2 in wheelbase. The front wheels were suspended independently, and steered by rack and pinion. Tyre size was 5.00-14 and price £383 for both models.

58C: **Morris** Oxford, Series MO, was introduced simultaneously with the Minor and featured the same basic styling. It was available only as a four-door Saloon, at £546. Engine was a 1476·5-cc (73·5 × 87 mm) side-valve Four, developing 41 bhp at 4200 rpm, driving through a four-speed gearbox with column shift. Like the Minor, the car had IFS with torsion bars and unitary body-cum-chassis construction.

59A: **Morris** Six, Series MS, was the Company's third new car for 1949. Priced at £672, this model had the same bodyshell as the Oxford (q.v.) but a longer bonnet, accommodating a 65-bhp six-cylinder OHC engine, and a vertical radiator grille. Wheelbase of the Oxford and Six was 8 ft 1 in and 9 ft 2 in respectively.

59B: **Riley** 2½-Litre RMD Drophead Coupé was produced from September 1948, until 1951. It cost £1215 and was based on the 2½-Litre Saloon (£1225; see 1948). In addition there were the three-seater Roadster at £1125 and the 1½-Litre Saloon at £913. The Roadster had steering-column mounted gearshift until January 1950, when it became a two-seater with centrally mounted remote control lever, like the other models.

59A Morris Six

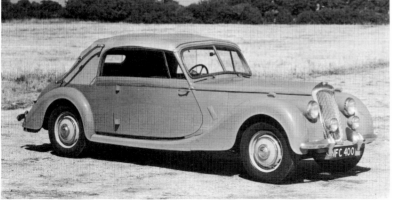

59B Riley 2½-Litre

59C Rolls-Royce Silver Wraith

59C: **Rolls-Royce** Silver Wraith 4¼-Litre Touring Limousine by Hooper, which cost £6068 and was the most expensive model in the 1949 catalogue. July saw the introduction of the smaller export-only Silver Dawn, which had the steel saloon body of the 'standard' Bentley (q.v.). It was not until late in 1953 that the Silver Dawn became readily available on the home market, by which time it had undergone several detail modifications.

1949

60A Rover Sixty and Seventy-Five

60B Rover Land-Rover

The SM *1500*

A modern motor-car of dignity, style and perfect balance created for the motorist who wants something better. One and a half litre—seating 5-6 in real comfort.

SINGER MOTORS LIMITED · BIRMINGHAM AND COVENTRY · ENGLAND

60C Singer SM1500

60A : **Rover** P3 Series was continued unchanged from 1949 (*q.v.*), in four- and six-cylinder form. The Seventy-Five was superseded in September by the P4 Series, which was entirely new with the main exception of the six-cylinder engine (in 1953 the Sixty was brought in line with the P4 Seventy-Five and another version, the P4 Ninety, added). A 1949 P3 six-light Saloon is shown.

60B : **Rover** introduced a 6/7-seater Station Wagon on the Land-Rover 80-in wheelbase chassis in October 1948. Not many were made, however, and this body style was discontinued in mid-1951.

60C : **Singer** SM1500 Saloon made its appearance in October 1948, and during 1949 the earlier Super Ten and Twelve Saloons were phased out. The SM1500 was placed into quantity production in mid-1949, alongside the Nine Roadster, and was an entirely new modernized model with coil-spring IFS, full-width body on longer wheelbase (separate) chassis. The body styling was not as elegant as most of its contenders in the $1\frac{1}{2}$-litre class. The price was £799.

61A Standard Vanguard

61A: **Standard** continued their well-selling Vanguard Series 20S (later known as Vanguard Phase I) Saloon, which had now become available on the home market. Like most British 1949 models, the car featured separate side lights from September (1950 model year). Phase I models remained in production, with periodical modifications, until 1953 when the beetle-back body was restyled and given a 'notch-back' rear end with projecting boot.

61B: **Sunbeam-Talbot** Ten and 2-Litre Saloons (*see* 1948) were superseded in the summer of 1948 by completely restyled models, the 80 and the 90, selling at £889 and £953 respectively. The very sleek bodywork, retaining the exclusive rear side window configuration, was by Thrupp & Maberly and was the same for both cars. The main difference was in the engine size, which was 1185 and 1944 cc like the preceding Ten and 2-Litre resp., but now with overhead valves and other modifications resulting in better performance, namely 47 bhp for the 80 and 64 for the 90.

61C: **Sunbeam-Talbot** 80 and 90 were available as two-door Convertible Coupé with three-position top. They cost £991 and £1055 respectively.

61D: **Sunbeam-Talbot** 80 and 90, dashboard and front compartment.

61C Sunbeam-Talbot 80/90

61B Sunbeam-Talbot 80/90

61D Sunbeam-Talbot 80/90

1949

62A Triumph 2000

62A: **Triumph** 2000 Roadster, Series 20TR, was in its last year. Compared with the preceding 1800 model (*see* 1948), the 1949 model had the same engine as the Standard Vanguard and also the latter's three-speed gearbox, replacing the earlier four-speed type. In all, about 4500 Roadsters were made and in recent years especially, this model has become a much sought after collector's car. Visible ahead of the boot lid handles is the hinged glass-panelled lid, which, when erected, formed a windscreen for the passengers in the dickey seat.

62B Vauxhall Velox

62B: **Vauxhall** 1949 models comprised the new Wyvern, Model LIX, and Velox, Model LIP, Saloons. The basic bodyshell was like the preceding Twelve, but front and rear end were new, and there were many other changes. The Wyvern differed from the Velox mainly in the following respects: four-cylinder 1442-cc engine (*v.* 2275-cc Six), wheels in body colour (*v.* cream), no bumper overriders and smaller-section tyres (5.00-16 *v.* 5.25 and later 5.90-16). For export to Australia special variants were produced, i.e. with a normal chassis frame for the mounting of Australian Saloon and Tourer bodywork (Wyvern LBX, Velox LBP).

63A: **Wolseley** 1949 programme consisted of two four-door Saloons, the Four-Fifty (shown) and the slightly longer Six-Eighty. They shared the bodywork and many other components with the Morris Oxford and Six, but had their own distinctive radiator grilles with the traditional illuminated radiator badge. The engines were similar in design, differing only in the number of cylinders and carburettors (Four-Fifty: single-carb. 51-bhp 1476-cc Four; Six-Eighty: twin-carb. 72-bhp 2215-cc Six). Bore and stroke were the same, 73·5 × 87 mm; both engines had an overhead camshaft. Prices were £704 and £767, wheelbase 8 ft 6 in and 9 ft 2 in respectively.

63A Wolseley Four-Fifty

63B: **Wolseley** produced a small number of pilot models of the new British Army FV1800 Series ¼-ton 4 × 4 vehicle, which was developed from the Nuffield 'Gutty' (*see* 1947) and powered by a Rolls-Royce B40 petrol engine. In one British Military publication the vehicle was listed as 'FV1801 Wolseley B. Jeep'; it was also known as Wolseley GP Vehicle, 5-cwt, 4 × 4. The Austin-built Champ, which was the eventual quantity-production model, differed mainly in having restyled wings and stiffening ribs pressed in the bonnet and body side panels (*see The Observer's Military Vehicles Directory*—from 1945).

63B Wolseley 'Mudlark'

INDEX

SUMMARY OF MAJOR BRITISH CAR MAKES
1947-1949 (with dates of their existence)

AC	(from 1908)	MG	(from 1924)
Alvis	(1920–67)	Morgan	(from 1910)
Armstrong Siddeley	(1919–60)	Morris	(from 1913)
Austin	(from 1906)	Riley	(1898–1969)
Bentley	(from 1920)	Rolls-Royce	(from 1904)
Daimler	(from 1896)	Rover	(from 1904)
Ford	(from 1911)	Singer	(1905–70)
Hillman	(from 1907)	Standard	(1903–63)
Humber	(from 1898)	Sunbeam-Talbot	(1938–54)
Jaguar	(from 1932)	Triumph	(from 1923)
Jowett	(1906–54)	Vauxhall	(from 1903)
Lagonda	(1906–63)	Wolseley	(from 1911)
Lanchester	(1895–1956)		
Lea-Francis	(1904–60)*	* irregularly	

ACKNOWLEDGEMENTS

This book was compiled and written largely from historic source material in the library of the Olyslager Organisation, and in addition photographs were kindly provided or loaned by several manufacturers and organizations, notably:

AC Cars Ltd, Alvis Owner Club (Mr R. A. Cox), Aston Martin Owners Club Ltd (Mr A. A. Archer), British Leyland UK Ltd (Austin-Morris, Jaguar, Rover and Triumph Divisions), Chrysler UK Ltd, Ford Motor Company Ltd, and Vauxhall Motors Ltd.

ABBREVIATIONS

bhp brake horsepower
CR compression ratio
HP taxable horsepower (RAC rating)
IFS independent front suspension
OHC overhead camshaft (engine)
OHV overhead valves (engine)
PT purchase tax
q.v. quod vide (which see)
2LS two leading shoes (brakes)